Developing Management Skills

Needs and Trends in Irish Civil Service Management Practice

Developing Management Skills

Needs and Trends in Irish Civil Service Management Practice

Richard Boyle

© Institute of Public Administration 1995

ISBN 1 872002 77 3

All rights reserved. No part of this publication may be reproduced or transmitted in any form or by any means, electronic or mechanical, including photocopy, recording or any information storage and retrieval system, without permission in writing from the publisher.

Published by
Institute of Public Administration
57-61 Lansdowne Road
Dublin 4
Ireland

Cover design by Butler Claffey, Dún Laoghaire
Typeset by Institute of Public Administration, Dublin
Printed by ColourBooks Ltd, Dublin

CONTENTS

Tables viii
Figures ix
Acknowledgements x

Chapter 1: Introduction 1
1.1 Focus of the report 1
1.2 Study background and objectives 1
1.3 Research strategy 4
1.4 Study approach and report structure 4

Chapter 2: Recent developments in civil service 7
management practice in Ireland
2.1 Introduction 7
2.2 Recent reviews of Irish public 7
service management
2.3 Recent government initiatives in 19
public service management
2.4 Conclusions 29

Chapter 3: Key themes guiding civil service 30
management development
3.1 Introduction 30
3.2 A new focus on strategic management 30
3.3 Increasing devolution of authority and 32
responsibility from the central to the local level
3.4 Greater emphasis on managing for 33
performance

3.5	Emphasising quality of service to clients and citizens	35
3.6	Getting things done through other organisations	36
3.7	A move from procedural accountability to accountability for results	37

Chapter 4: Identifying the key roles of civil servants   39
4.1	Introduction	39
4.2	The civil servant as strategist	39
4.3	The civil servant as policy analyst	40
4.4	The civil servant as broker	41
4.5	The civil servant as people manager	43
4.6	The civil servant as information manager	45
4.7	The civil servant as financial manager	46
4.8	The civil servant as monitor/evaluator	48
4.9	The civil servant as change agent	49
4.10	Summary	50

Chapter 5: Towards a curriculum for management education and development for the Irish civil service   53
5.1	Introduction	53
5.2	An appropriate model for the knowledge base of management education in the Irish civil service	53
5.3	Topics for inclusion in a management education and development curriculum	58
5.4	Conclusions	64

Chapter 6: Developing a learning culture in the   65
           Irish civil service
6.1   Introduction   65
6.2   Generating, reinforcing and sustaining capacities   65
6.3   Creating and sustaining a learning organisation   68
6.4   Conclusions   78

References   79

Bibliography   86

TABLES

Table 1   Main features of administrative budget   22
             agreements in the Irish civil service

Table 2   Topics for inclusion in a management   59
             education and development curriculum

Table 3   Creating a learning climate focused   77
             on strategic management issues in the
             Department of Transport, Energy
             and Communications

FIGURES

Figure 1 Framework for the study 5

Figure 2 Framework for a strategic management process 28

Figure 3 The domains of public service organisations and their characteristics 56

Figure 4 A framework for capacity development 66

Figure 5 A learning cycle setting for skills and capacity development in organisations 73

ACKNOWLEDGEMENTS

This report was commissioned and funded by the Department of Finance, through its Committee for Administrative Research. I would like to thank the committee for its help and support, under the chairmanship of Paddy Moore.

Within the civil service, a large number of individuals were helpful in providing information and support. Eric Embleton (Department of Finance), a member of the Committee for Administrative Research, provided significant guidance and advice at various stages in the project. I would also like to particularly acknowledge the contribution of Brendan Tuohy (Department of Transport, Energy and Communications), who made many insightful comments and contributions to earlier drafts of the report. Others who made time for discussions and whom I would like to thank are: Joe Boyle (Civil Service Commission); John Buckley (Office of the Comptroller and Auditor General); John Dully (Department of Tourism and Trade); Josephine Feehily (Office of the Revenue Commissioners); Paul Haran (Department of Enterprise and Employment); Seamus Healy (Department of Agriculture, Food and Forestry); Michael Kelly (Department of Health); Joe McGovern (Department of Finance); David O'Callaghan (Department of Defence); Caomhín O hUiginn (Department of Justice); Dave Power (Department of Social Welfare); Seamus Rogers (Valuation Office); Eddie Sullivan (Department of Social Welfare); and Catherine Treacy (Land Registry).

Within the Institute, I would like to thank Pat Hall for his advice and encouragement. Tony McNamara and Jim O'Donnell, along with the rest of the publications section, provided excellent support and advice. Finally, Carolyn Gormley and Annmarie Kelly provided excellent administrative support throughout the project.

Richard Boyle
April 1995.

1
Introduction

1.1 Focus of the report

This report on skills and capacity development in the Irish civil service was commissioned by the Department of Finance through its Committee for Administrative Research. It focuses on the changing context in which civil servants are having to manage their activities, and the consequent need for new skills and capacities if civil servants are to maintain an effective role on behalf of the state. The study is based on a review of the literature and on a series of interviews with senior civil servants. The report offers suggestions to civil servants who are involved in the increasing professionalisation of the Irish civil service.

1.2 Study background and objectives

Management in the public sector in many OECD countries has changed radically in the past ten to fifteen years.[1] A new approach to governance, labelled the 'new public management', has come to prominence in a number of countries.[2] The approach differs from traditional public administration based on bureaucratic control mechanisms. Alternative control mechanisms, such as contracting-out, or greater devolution and team-based work, are promoted. Senior managers are being given greater discretion in the running of their departments. An explicit focus on outputs and results is emphasised. As a result, significant changes are taking place in the structure, composition and tasks of the civil service.

In Ireland, there is a recognition at both political and administrative levels that changes in civil service management practice are needed if the civil service is to continue to provide an effective service to citizens. In this context, a number of initiatives have been taken in recent years that are affecting the running of the civil service.

Information technology is increasingly influential in how administration operates. The three-year administrative budgets for government departments are in their second round. The Comptroller and Auditor General (Amendment) Act 1993 gives increased impetus to value-for-money practices and procedures. The strategic management initiative aims to make government departments more efficient, accountable and user-friendly.[3]

Further changes are on the way. A *Government of Renewal*, the policy agreement between Fine Gael, the Labour Party and Democratic Left which forms the basis for the government appointed in December 1994 refers specifically in its opening sentences to the need for change, where the parties pledge themselves to:

> ... the reform of our institutions at national and local level to provide service, accountability, transparency and freedom of information. In so doing we are committed to extending the opportunities for democratic participation by citizens in all aspects of public life.[4]

In an interview at the beginning of 1995, the Minister for Finance, Mr Quinn indicated: 'I want nothing less than the total reform and modernisation of the civil service to prepare for the twenty-first century.'[5]

These developments place new demands on civil servants. In particular, there are increasing calls for the professionalisation of the civil service. One former senior official in the Department of Finance indicates a need for:

> ... a practical recognition of the fact that public administration is a profession and not just an expression of common sense and experience catalysed by intelligence. Such a recognition would involve a substantial programme of training and education in public administration and a commitment to employing

the trained professional in the public service, especially the civil service.[6]

But what route will this professionalisation of the civil service take? Many commentators have labelled the changes which have taken place, and those proposed, as a move towards a more 'managerial' civil service, away from the traditional concept of public administration. Yet definitions of public service management vary, from those who see it essentially as taking private sector skills and methods and applying them in the public sector to those who interpret it as a 're-labelling' of the traditional skills and capacities of civil servants. As a relatively new discipline, public service management has, as yet, no firm 'territory' it can call its own.

Neither are the implications of a move to public service management, in terms of the new demands to be placed on civil servants, fully understood or explored.

It was in the light of such issues that this study was set up. The objectives were that the study would seek to:

(a) Identify and outline significant developments in the civil service environment in recent years, both in Ireland and internationally, and the implications of these developments.[7]

(b) Explore the varying definitions of public service management and arrive at a clarification of the term in the context of public sector developments in Ireland.

(c) Identify and outline the key skills and capacities needed by civil servants to operate effectively in the public service, with a view to informing the curriculum for management education and development in the public sector.

(d) Outline the implications for skills acquisition in the civil service, particularly in terms of training and development, education and recruitment requirements.

1.3 Research strategy

Two main sources were used to gather information for this study:

(a) *A review of the literature.* In this way, a general picture of the problems and issues associated with skills and capacity development was built up. Also, something was learned of developments in the public sectors of other countries.

(b) *Semi-structured interviews.* Interviews were held with a range of senior civil servants responsible for various aspects of skills and capacity development in the civil service. In particular, fifteen assistant secretaries, or equivalent grades, were interviewed (some more than once), to ensure that the study incorporated a view from within the civil service at a senior level as to likely future trends and requirements.

Data was collected during 1994 and early 1995. Reports, files and other documentary sources were also examined as appropriate.

1.4 Study approach and report structure

In order to consider skills and capacity development, it is useful to have a conceptual framework for the study. This is set out in Figure 1. Essentially, the study starts off by reviewing the context for the subject under scrutiny, establishing the pressures for change and the changes which are taking place in civil service management in Ireland (Chapter 2). It then identifies the various themes arising from these changes that impact on skills and capacity development at a departmental level (Chapter 3). The next stage is to investigate skills and capacity requirements at the level of the individual civil

Framework for the study

Current issues in civil service management practice in Ireland	*What is the context for skills and capacity development?*

↓

Themes arising from the current issues	*What are the organisational implications?*

↓

Developing existing and new roles for civil servants	*What skills and capacities are needed at the level of the individual?*
Developing a curriculum for management education and development in the civil service	*What topics need study to inform skills and capacity development?*

↓

Generating, reinforcing and sustaining capacities	*What are the implications for organisational learning?*

servant (Chapter 4), and to identify the topics to be covered in developing a curriculum for management education and development in the civil service (Chapter 5). Finally, the implications for selection and development, appraisal and reward, and organisational design and communications are explored (Chapter 6).

2
Recent developments in civil service management practice in Ireland

2.1 Introduction

In this chapter, recent reviews of public service management practice are set out, and the implications of these reviews explored. Following on from this, recent government initiatives, aimed at improving civil service management, and established in the light of the criticisms and comments made in the reviews, are explored.

2.2 Recent reviews of Irish public service management

There have been a number of reviews in recent years which have commented on how we manage the public sector, and in particular on civil service management. Recent National Economic and Social Council (NESC) reports *A strategy for the nineties*[8] and *A strategy for competitiveness, growth and employment*[9] have given an overview of civil service management as it relates to the management of public expenditure. Also, with regard to specific sectors, the report of the industrial policy review group (the Culliton report)[10], the education white paper[11] and the health strategy *Shaping a healthier future*[12] all comment on the role government departments have played and should play in ensuring effective management. Each of these reports gives an insight into the current state of public service management and the main issues to be faced in coming years.

NESC reviews

In both *A strategy for the nineties* and *A strategy for competitiveness, growth and employment,* one of the issues the NESC discuss is the management of public expenditure. They indicate that management of the public sector is important in securing an effective strategy for economic and social policy.

The NESC reports point out that the management of public expenditure covers both the *planning and control* of public expenditure. In particular, the NESC distinguishes between strategic planning and control and operational planning and control. At the operational level, the objectives of government expenditure, their design and specification, and the level at which they are carried out, are taken as given. At the strategic level, however, issues such as the establishment and specification of objectives, choosing between alternative policy instruments to achieve objectives, and allocating resources between programmes are all issues for decision.

The reports identify institutional difficulties when it comes to aligning expenditure with macroeconomic requirements and changing priorities at the strategic level. *A strategy for the nineties* states:

> In Ireland, as in most other countries, public expenditure management revolves around spending departments, agencies and their expenditure programmes. Each of these participants in the budgetary process endeavours to protect their own programmes. There is, therefore, an incentive for all programme and agency managers to push against the overall limit or resource constraint. There is no incentive or mechanism within the institutional structure for one programme to compete with another.

NESC explores the case for altering the system of public expenditure management to involve a 'resource envelope', within which there would be freedom to identify priorities and allocate resources. However, the council does not advocate the adoption of any particular system based on the 'resource envelope' premise. They also raise questions about the ability of individual departments to think and act strategically, voicing some concern in this regard:

> The suggestion that central planning departments should concentrate on the allocation of resources to reflect broad priorities, with decision-making on specific programme choice delegated down, raises a fundamental question about the ability of individual departments to take a strategic perspective and allocate resources to reflect this perspective. Unfortunately the evidence is not very encouraging.

The reasons for the disappointing performance of government departments in strategic management are unclear, according to NESC. However, one reason mentioned is that agencies often: (a) have staff whose qualifications and expertise outstrip that of the parent department, and (b) have long standing and extremely strong autonomy, thus making strategic management extremely difficult.

NESC also raise the crucial role of strategic thinking in government departments in the context of Ireland's relationship with the European Union. In a review of Ireland's comparative performance in the European Community, the council argues that the co-ordination of individual departmental responses can only be achieved if a strategic perspective is adopted.[13] The council also indicates that departments must be capable of producing arguments of the highest quality in order to ensure that the Irish perspective is included in European issues and in the evolution of the European Union.

At the operational management level, in both *A strategy for the nineties* and *A strategy for competitiveness, growth and employment*, NESC examine a number of measures taken to improve the efficiency and effectiveness of public expenditure:

- *Direct input controls*, notably constraints on manpower. Whilst effective in terms of restraining public expenditure, such measures are viewed as giving rise to a number of problems, such as their impact on manpower intensive services, areas of high-turnover, and the fact that they affect front-line staff more than support staff. The consequent need for such retrenchment measures to be accompanied by managerial efforts to redeploy resources in line with policy priorities is stressed.

- *Improving financial management*, centred around more decentralised procedures for taking executive decisions and more delegation of decision taking. For this: '...individual managers need clear objectives (and, at a lower level, clear tasks) coupled with responsibility for good use of resources provided to each in a delegated budget.'

- *External monitoring* of the efficiency and effectiveness of government expenditure. The role of private sector input into efficiency and effectiveness reviews and external monitoring by the government's auditor are both cited as noteworthy developments internationally.

- *Exposure to competitive sources*, to test the cost-efficiency of government activity. Here, the NESC view is that competition is the key dimension to ensuring efficiency. The core policy option chosen, therefore, is one of ensuring effective competition where possible.

Culliton report

The industrial policy review group (Culliton group) was established by the Minister for Industry and Commerce in June 1991 to carry out a fundamental examination of industrial policy and public policy generally as it affects industrial development. One of the issues covered by the group and highlighted in their report is the institutional arrangements for delivering industrial services and for formulating and monitoring policy. The group took a critical look at the role of the then Department of Industry and Commerce.[14] Whilst the comments of the group are limited to this one department, many of the topics which the group identify and address would generally be recognised as common across a wide range of government departments.

Several key issues are identified by the Culliton group in their report with regard to departmental management: departmental policy formulation; managing the relationship with executive agencies; decentralisation of administrative and operational functions; and information needs.

Departmental policy formulation. The Culliton group are quite clear in their views on policy formulation:

> It has been widely remarked that the Irish administrative system, in general, is weak in policy formulation. Either as cause or effect, it has become preoccupied with administration and crisis management. This requires change.

The Culliton group see two functions in the policy role which should be played by the Department of Industry and Commerce: (a) the development of industrial policy, and (b) the monitoring of the internal and external environment to allow policy to be updated. In practice, they saw the department too dependent on ad hoc in-depth reviews of industrial policy, drawing heavily on external expertise. Consequently in their report, the Culliton group state: 'It is essential that the department develops an internal capacity for fundamental policy review and evaluation. The department requires significant strengthening in this respect.'

Managing the relationship with executive agencies. The Culliton group report that in the absence of a clear policy direction from the department, the various executive agencies charged with implementing aspects of industrial policy (such as the IDA and An

11

Bord Tráchtála) have in practice developed their own policy objectives, which are not necessarily in harmony with each other. Thus the agencies themselves play a central role in determining policy for the sectors for which they have responsibility. Whilst this is not necessarily in itself a bad thing, the absence of strong co-ordination from the centre is seen as a weakness that can lead to conflict and divergence of practice and, consequently, poor value for money from industrial promotion expenditure.

To overcome this problem, the Culliton group recommend that clear, national policy objectives be set for industrial development. These objectives should cover not only those executive agencies under the responsibility of the Department of Industry and Commerce, but also other areas of government activity significantly affecting industrial development. The group recognise that this would require new organisational arrangements both within and external to the department. For those areas under the direct control of the department, the recommendation is that:

> The department should set specific and measurable policy objectives for the boards and management of the industrial development agencies and then let them get on with the job. These objectives should be agreed with the boards of the executive agencies and form the basis for an assessment of the performance of the agencies and the rational allocation of resources.

As well as the department avoiding becoming involved in the day-to-day minutiae of state enterprises, the Moriarty task force, established by the government to advise on how best the Culliton report recommendations could be implemented, recommend that submissions by state enterprises to government departments should be dealt with promptly and that each sponsoring department should review its procedures for expeditiously processing proposals from state enterprises so that commercial opportunities are not missed.[15]

Decentralisation of administrative and operational functions. Notwithstanding the difficulties that have arisen in the policy formulation and control arrangements between the department and the industrial development executive agencies, the Culliton group conclude that there are a number of administrative functions which the department carries out that would be better performed by self-funding para-statal bodies, under broad policy direction from the department. The Companies Office and Patents Office are cited as executive functions which could be separated from the department.

The rationale for this recommendation is that it would bring benefits both (a) to the department, who as a result could concentrate more effectively on its policy-making responsibilities, and (b) to the decentralised functions, which on a day-to-day executive basis would be freed from the constraints of a government department.

The Moriarty task force, rather than opt for the creation of separate executive agencies, recommend that decisions should be taken with a view to achieving a commercial, services-oriented structure for the Companies Office and Patents Office, and this approach has been endorsed by the government.

Information needs. The Culliton group identify the central role of information in policy making and evaluation:

> An essential requirement for policy formulation is to have an adequate industry-related information base – both statistical and other – available to enable officials to assess the effectiveness or otherwise of existing policy. Such an information base has been substantially lacking.

The report therefore highlights the establishment of an adequate industry-related information base as a key task to be co-ordinated by the department but also involving the co-operation of executive agencies both within and outside government. To undertake this task the group states that the data-gathering and analysis skills in the department should be strengthened.

Education white paper

A recent OECD review of education in Ireland indicated that the Irish educational system was over centralised:

> ... although a small system, it has the same administrative apparatus and faces the same problems of control, management and monitoring as large systems ... The schools are locally managed ... but in so far as the exercise of its specific powers are concerned, the Department of Education functions like a ... highly centralised bureaucracy.[16]

The green paper on education produced by the government in 1992 recognises this point, and states that one of the shortcomings of the Irish education system is that 'The education system is over-centralised, with even the smallest decisions on everyday administration taken by the Department of Education. This approach, as well as being inefficient, distracts the department from its central task of strategic policy-making.' The green paper was followed by a national debate on educational policy, focusing on a national education convention held in October 1993. A white paper on education was produced in April 1995.[17]

The solution put forward in the white paper to overcome this problem of centralisation is radical devolution of decision-making and responsibility in the education system. The principle to be applied is that everything that can be administered effectively at individual school level should be done there. This will shift decisively from the Department of Education the responsibility for day-to-day administration, freeing it to concentrate on strategy issues allied to policy-making.

The green paper spelt out the main tasks that the Department of Education should focus on:

- *Formulating strategic policy.* This includes policy development and the monitoring of the education system at a national level, and the closer linking of educational research with policy-making.

- *Assuring educational quality standards and efficiency throughout the system.* This entails developing and maintaining national standards of quality, and ensuring the efficient and effective management of the system.

- *Overall budgetary responsibility.* This incorporates the equitable allocation of resources on the basis of a well-defined budgetary framework.

- *Identifying and responding to special needs.* This involves needs identification and assessment and ensuring support for those in need of special help and attention.

The white paper places great stress on quality, and in particular the role of the department, through the inspectorate, in achieving and maintaining quality. The focus of the inspectorate is to be on the general evaluation of schools, the dissemination of good practice, and contribution to policy formulation.

Health strategy

The health strategy *Shaping a healthier future* which was introduced by the Minister for Health in 1994 aims at re-orienting the health system towards improving the effectiveness of the health and personal social services. Part of this re-orientation is to be achieved by reshaping the management and organisational structures which provide the framework for service delivery, including re-defining the role of the Department of Health.

Three key principles are identified as underpinning the health strategy: equity, quality of service and accountability. These principles affect the development of health service delivery and the consequent demands placed on health service personnel:

> *Equity* centres around the concept of actual *need* for services rather than ability to pay or geographic location. It is concerned with variations in the health status of different groups in society and how these might be addressed.
>
> *Quality of service* concerns both (a) the *technical quality* of treatment or care so that the best possible outcome is achieved, and (b) the *consumer's perception of quality* of the services he or she receives.
>
> *Accountability* includes: legal and financial accountability arrangements; the need for those providing services to accept responsibility for the achievement of agreed objectives; and mechanisms to ensure that those with decision-making powers are adequately accountable to the consumers of the services.

If the health service is to improve equity, quality of service and accountability, the health strategy recognises that organisational structures must ensure that the responsibilities of various organisations working in the health sector are clearly stated and understood. The strategy consequently sets out the role it envisages for the various agencies. For the Department of Health, the strategy states that while the Minister for Health will continue to have ultimate responsibility to the Oireachtas for all health services, his department will no longer be involved in the detailed management of individual services. The principal responsibilities of the department in the future are set out in the health strategy:

- Advising and supporting the minister in determining national policy.

- Strategic planning and management at a national level.

- Advising the Minister for Health and the government in its determination of the annual health estimate.

- Determining the financial allocation of the regional health authorities.

- Determining the overall personnel policies within which health authorities function.

- Monitoring and evaluating the service and financial performance of the authorities against national objectives and standards.

- Identifying and supporting the introduction of more effective management practices.

- Supporting the minister in his functions in relation to other statutory bodies under his aegis.

Drawing together these functions, it can be seen that the Department of Health's new role will give prominence to three major areas of activity:

- *Strategic thinking and planning.* The department will have overall responsibility for the health gain and social gain approach outlined in the strategy. Health gain is concerned with health status and social gain with broader aspects of the quality of life. In order to secure the benefits of this approach, the department will need to be able to: take an overview of developments in the environment as they impact on health need, develop and articulate priority areas for action, and ensure that decisions on priorities and resource allocation are made in an open and objective manner.

- *Direction giving.* For those agencies under the control of the department, notably the health authorities, the department will be involved in ensuring that the priorities identified and outlined at national level in the strategic management process are carried through, in the context of resource allocation decisions. This will involve assessing and monitoring the strategic plans for the health authorities, and giving clear guidance on issues where consistency is needed.

    For those private sector agencies operating in the health area, where the department does not have any direct control function, and for other sectors which impact on health, such as social welfare, agriculture and the environment, the department will need to ensure the coordination of activities by influencing developments in the various sectors and liaising closely with the relevant agencies. It will be responsible for ensuring a co-ordinated multi-sectoral health policy involving the key policy areas that impact upon health.

- *Monitoring and evaluation.* An essential element of health strategy is the transformation of the basis on which resource choices are made. The emphasis is on moving away from decisions based on unsubstantiated claims, or in favour of those who shout loudest, towards enhancing the role of evaluation of health care needs and the relative effectiveness of available responses to different forms of need. In this context, one of the key roles for the department identified in the strategy is the evaluation of the services and financial performance of the regional health authorities against national objectives. Effectiveness and quality of service will be crucial dimensions in this performance measurement role. The strategy states that:

    > As part of the restructuring of the Department of Health, which will follow from the devolution of some of its present work, arrangements will have to be made to support a structured annual performance review of health

authorities. The department will also support and encourage the development of suitable arrangements within the health authorities to enable them to review the performance of their own costs centres and the agencies providing services on their behalf.

2.3 Recent government initiatives in public service management

The government have taken a number of initiatives over the last few years which are aimed at improving civil service management practice in the light of the criticisms and comments made in the reviews of public service management which have taken place. Of particular note are four major initiatives which over the coming years are likely to impact significantly on the practice of management in the civil service: the exploitation of information technology in the civil service; administrative budgets; the Comptroller and Auditor General (Amendment) Act 1993; and the strategic management initiative.

The exploitation of information technology in the civil service

The use of information technology in the civil service has been actively pursued for many years now. In recent years, the focus has been on the potential role of information technology in influencing the operation and capabilities of government departments. Managerial autonomy and accountability are issues which departments are now facing, and ones which require sophisticated information systems to be in place to support their development. Also, information technology has been a major catalyst facilitating the decentralisation of civil servants from Dublin to regional centres.

From 1986, departments have been required to draw up formal annual and multi-annual information technology plans.

Increasingly, these plans are having a major bearing on the determination of financial provisions for IT and on the prioritisation of activities. The process can also be seen as the precursor of the strategic management initiative, as it requires departments to start from the management of information and resources rather than from assessing technological options. Guidelines produced by the Central IT Services section of the Department of Finance indicate that the IT plan should be firmly linked to the aims and objectives of departmental priority areas.

Recently, a review has taken place of the benefits achieved from information technology in the civil service.[18] This review found that the most widespread benefits of IT systems are in the productivity category. IT was also found to have enabled departments to remain competitive with those organisations that either they or their clients do business with. There was some disappointment, however, at the lack of impact IT had on management performance and organisational effectiveness. Factors identified as influential in restricting IT to a relatively narrow impact in the civil service to date include:

- The absence in the civil service generally of a 'change climate' and the associated risk-taking.

- The initial system installed in a department or section may have been sponsored by an enthusiastic user manager, but (s)he may not have been at a sufficiently high level to carry forward the necessary expansion either upwards or outwards within the organisation.

- There may have been no pressing business need or strong imperative to extend computerisation to other areas of the organisation.

Senior management commitment is seen as the key element that can prevent or overcome these weaknesses. This is not so much a commitment to IT, but a commitment to quality and an openness to change as an essential element in achieving quality and improving organisational effectiveness.

Administrative budgets

Administrative budgets cover the running costs of government departments and offices.[19] They include such items as pay, travel and subsistence, consultancy and information technology. Administrative budgets were introduced as a new system of budgetary allocation for running costs in government departments in 1991. Under the system, budgets for running costs are determined in advance for a three-year period, and reduced in real terms over that time.[20] Within the agreed amounts, departmental managers have greater freedom than under the old system to allocate and spend resources. There are two key objectives of each agreement:

- To bring about a real reduction or stability in the cost of running departments over the period of the agreement.

- To improve departmental efficiency and effectiveness through:

    - delegating greater authority from the Minister for Finance to the departmental minister in relation to administrative expenditure and related matters, and

    - encouraging and facilitating the delegating of greater authority to line managers in departments in relation to administrative expenditure.

The main features of administrative budget agreements are set out in Table 1. The system of administrative budgeting is seen as a major initiative in the Irish civil service:

> The effects of the budgets go far beyond the visible changes in accounting and sanctioning procedures. The

TABLE 1

Main Features of Administrative Budget Agreements in the Irish Civil Service

- Provisions set for each year of a three-year period

- Commitment by departmental minister to contain running costs within the agreed provisions

- Commitment by Minister for Finance to meet increases in unit costs arising as a direct result of decisions by Minister for Finance

- Reductions in costs of 2 per cent per annum in real terms over the period of the agreement, or alternatively no reductions provided departments guarantee to resource workload changes from within their administrative budget

- Departments given delegated authority to incur administrative expenditure subject to certain conditions

- Allowance of virement of funds between budget subheads subject to an upper limit

- Permission to carry forward savings from one year to the next subject to an overall limit

- Joint departmental/Department of Finance Monitoring Group established to oversee the operation of the agreement

- Aim of gradual transfer of greater authority to line managers for administrative expenditure

- Aim to devise quantitative indicators to assess the effectiveness of administrative expenditure in meeting programme objectives

new system will profoundly affect the way the civil service is managed. Managers will now have considerable freedom to manage within the budgets allocated to them. The slogan 'let the managers manage' may be an apt description of the new process. Managers will have to determine their priorities and allocate resources accordingly. They can no longer pass that responsibility to someone else.[21]

The general perception among managers in line departments is that the impact of the first three-year cycle of administrative budgets has been fairly limited. Administrative budgets as they stand are seen as a useful first step in changing the culture of the civil service, creating greater cost consciousness, but not having much effect to date on performance. With staffing costs accounting for some seventy per cent of administrative budgets, and senior management posts and pay rates still under the control of the Department of Finance, the system is seen as giving limited discretion to departmental managers. Also, the requirement in the first three-year cycle to reduce administrative costs by two per cent per annum was viewed as restricting the scope of the scheme, and orienting the scheme towards cost-cutting rather than enhancing effectiveness. Administrative budgets are primarily seen as an input control mechanism. Also, the system as it stands does not address the relationship between administrative and programme expenditure.

However, despite these comments, the general view is that the concept of administrative budgets and increased devolution of responsibility to line departments is one to be supported and encouraged. Also, it needs to be recognised that administrative budgeting is still at an early stage of development. In particular, some departments have faced difficulties due to the lack of adequate financial management and reporting systems. The financial management systems (FMS) and personnel administration systems (PAS) now being put in place in departments should provide a support service to enable the more effective management of resources. Similarly, the strategic management initiative, by focusing departments on priorities, objectives and targets, should help in providing a link between resource inputs and the outputs delivered by departments.

The Comptroller and Auditor General (Amendment) Act 1993

The Comptroller and Auditor General (Amendment) Act 1993 consolidates and updates the existing statutory provisions in relation to the role of the C&AG. The Act also extends the range and scope of the C&AGs functions to take account of international developments in national audit and extends the accountability role of the C&AG.

The Act gives the C&AG a particular role in relation to *value for money* auditing. Section 9 of the Act provides the C&AG with a value for money (VFM) remit '... the purpose of which is to provide the Dáil with independent assurance as to the economy, efficiency and effectiveness with which a department has used its resources in discharging its function.'[22] The C&AG has two main responsibilities with regard to VFM auditing:

- He is empowered *directly* to assess the economy and efficiency of resource use by departments.

- He is empowered to examine the adequacy of the management systems, procedures and practices employed by departments to enable them to evaluate the effectiveness of their own operations.

A recent review of the Act sets out the main implications of VFM auditing:

> Section 9 of the Act will enable the C&AG to develop further his recent initiative of producing project audit reports dealing with specific programmes and operations. It will enable him to form opinions as to how well

managed departments and other bodies audited by him are. He will be expressly empowered to make comparisons between different bodies and operations and to draw attention to inadequacies where he finds them, but on a more positive note he will be able to cite examples of effective systems and good management which might repay study and evaluation by management in other bodies.[23]

In a guidance note produced for government departments, the C&AG's Office sets out what it sees as departmental responsibility for effectiveness evaluation. The note states that a department should aim to have:

- Clear statements of its objectives and the criteria to assess performance in relation to those objectives.

- Procedures for examining the appropriateness of policy instruments applied to implement government policy, particularly the merits and demerits of each policy instrument option from a VFM perspective.

- Well defined responsibility for ensuring periodic critical scrutiny of performance, reporting to decision-makers, and for the initiation of appropriate corrective action, if warranted.

- Management information systems capable of delivering reliable and timely data to underpin the system of performance review.

- Adequate staff training and access to such expert advice as is needed to enable the department to meet its performance review obligations.[24]

Responsibility for the operation of effectiveness evaluation systems, practices and procedures, rests with senior and line management in each department. Current thinking in the C&AG's

Office is that in the larger executive-oriented departments at least, the establishment of a small central support unit with responsibility for co-ordinating departmental effectiveness evaluation activities will help line managers meet their VFM requirements. Internal audit is also seen as having a key role to play in highlighting areas within departments which would benefit from in-depth scrutinies. An internal audit network has recently been set up, to provide a forum for the exchange of views, ideas and experience of civil servants involved in internal audit.

The Strategic Management Initiative

On 22nd February 1994 the then Taoiseach, Albert Reynolds, TD, made a speech to ministers and departmental secretaries on the theme of developing strategic management in the Irish public service. In the speech, he announced the establishment of a strategic management initiative (SMI) in the civil service. Among the main points highlighted in the speech are the following:

- Each department secretary and head of office must put in place a process of strategic management.

- A first step in this process is the establishment of a strategic statement and action plan, within six months.

- Three key areas are to be addressed:

    - making a contribution to national development
    - providing an excellent service to the public
    - ensuring the effective use of resources.

- Senior management in each department and office must collectively review and analyse the factors affecting their organisations.

- A co-ordinating group of secretaries will bring department strategies together and recommend changes to ensure that the total is more than the sum of the parts.

A subsequent note produced by the Department of Finance outlines the framework within which departmental strategic statements and action plans are to be devised and progressed. The note states that if the initiative is to be successful, the process must, among other things:

- have the support of, and be driven by, the top management of the department
- be underpinned by a strategic thinking approach and an openness on the part of the department to taking a fundamental look at itself
- be supported by the necessary structures and systems to underpin successful implementation.[25]

It is envisaged that these actions will arise through a series of stages in the strategic management process, as set out in Figure 2. Essentially, the process involves reflection on the organisation's mandate, development of a view of where it wishes to be positioned in the future, the strategies, systems and structures needed to be put in place to achieve this desired state, and constant monitoring and feedback to maintain the process.

Whilst there was some slippage with regard to the six-month deadline, nearly all departments and offices had produced a strategic statement and action plan by the end of 1994.

As a strategic management *process*, rather than a mechanism for producing strategic plans, the SMI is encouraging departments to investigate their organisational structures and procedures in the light of their strategic review and analysis. The aim is to stimulate each department's thinking on how best to mediate its relationship with its working environment.

Framework for Strategic Management Process

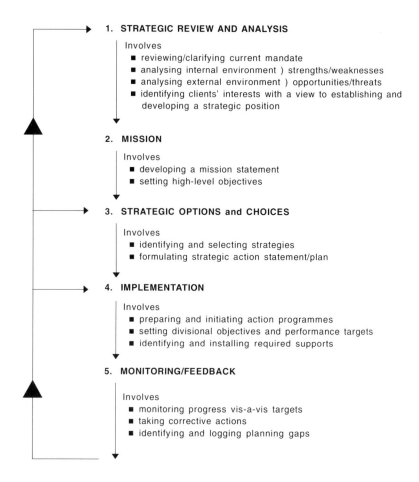

1. **STRATEGIC REVIEW AND ANALYSIS**

   Involves
   - reviewing/clarifying current mandate
   - analysing internal environment) strengths/weaknesses
   - analysing external environment) opportunities/threats
   - identifying clients' interests with a view to establishing and developing a strategic position

2. **MISSION**

   Involves
   - developing a mission statement
   - setting high-level objectives

3. **STRATEGIC OPTIONS and CHOICES**

   Involves
   - identifying and selecting strategies
   - formulating strategic action statement/plan

4. **IMPLEMENTATION**

   Involves
   - preparing and initiating action programmes
   - setting divisional objectives and performance targets
   - identifying and installing required supports

5. **MONITORING/FEEDBACK**

   Involves
   - monitoring progress vis-a-vis targets
   - taking corrective actions
   - identifying and logging planning gaps

Taken from 'Framework for the development of a strategic management process in the civil service', a note issued to each government department and office by the Department of Finance, 1994.

The role of the co-ordinating group is of importance, particularly with regard to ensuring the integration of the various departmental strategies. To facilitate this task, some long-term vision for the government would set the context for departmental strategies and their integration. One possible approach is that the government as a whole set strategic result areas (SRAs), which are translated into key result areas (KRAs) for each department.[26]

It is too early as yet to judge the impact of the strategic management initiative. However, the Minister for Finance, Mr Quinn, has indicated that he intends to continue the initiative and give it a high priority. A minister of state, Ms Avril Doyle, TD, has been appointed with special responsibility to advance the SMI, an indication of continuing political commitment to and interest in the initiative.

2.4 Conclusions

The preceding sections indicate some of the forces that have been acting for change in the civil service, and some of the initiatives which have arisen partly in response to these forces. The environment within which the manager in the civil service operates is becoming more complex. This changing environment within which the civil servant works sets the scene for an exploration of the key issues to be tackled in civil service management, and the consequent implications for skills and capacity development in civil servants.

3
Key themes guiding civil service management development

3.1 Introduction

Certain key themes can be found in the reviews of public service management which have occurred and in the government initiatives to improve public service management. These themes reflect the changes that are thought to be desirable in public service management. They have implications for the development of future skills and capacities in civil service managers. The themes explored here are: strategic management; devolution; performance management; quality of service; inter-organisational working; and accountability for results. The focus of this chapter is at the departmental level. The implications for individual civil servants are explored in the next chapter.

3.2 A new focus on strategic management

Perhaps the strongest message arising from the reviews and government initiatives is the need to develop and enhance strategic management capabilities in government departments. There is a need for each department to be able to articulate a strategy for the sector for which it has responsibility. Also, each department must be able to develop a strategy for organisational change in its own organisation. The strategic perspective has both an internal and an external focus. There is a perceived weakness in the ability of departments to take a strategic perspective, most notably articulated in the NESC *A strategy for the nineties* report. The strategic management initiative is aimed at overcoming this weakness.

The strategic management initiative recognises a crucial distinction: between *process* and *plans*. Thus whilst the production of a strategic plan is a key element in strategic management, it is not the whole story. This is to avoid the danger of the plan becoming the sole focus of attention. If this happens, the end result may be a document which is large and full of voluminous data, but which does not impact on day-to-day management practices. Also, a plan is only of relevance to those issues which can be planned for and where some stability in the environment is likely to enable the plan to proceed. For many strategic issues, a plan may not be the best way to tackle them. Issues may emerge from unexpected quarters or from political imperatives, and have to be dealt with as the situation at the time demands. This is where a well developed strategic management process, capable of identifying such issues and developing approaches to their management, comes into the picture.

As well as developing a sound strategic management process, it is critical that departments ensure that strategic management activities are 'owned' by senior and line management and not seen as the preserve of strategic planning specialists. Strategic thinking needs to be influenced by and to influence managers who are supervising and delivering services. But this places particular pressures on already hard-pressed managers. There is still a role for strategic planners, but as facilitators and integrators rather than as 'doers'. The job of the strategic planner is to help managers work through the strategic management process, providing analytical back-up, support and guidance. Planners also need to help set out the practical actions which must be taken to translate strategies into practice.

The strategic management capabilities required of departments can be grouped around three key characteristics of strategic management:

- It has a perspective which is *long-term*, exposes *choices*, is guided by *political values* and is *grounded* in the *environment* rather than the organisation.

- It identifies issues to be dealt with, values to be expressed or activities to be undertaken which are *beyond the normal way of working* because of structure, process, culture or resource limitations.

- It is concerned with *organisational change* and establishing new ways of working.[27]

3.3 Increasing devolution of authority and responsibility from the central to the local level

The principle of devolution runs through the reviews and government initiatives, and is crucial for effective strategic management. Devolved managerial structures can take two forms: (a) *internal devolution*, where operational management is devolved to internal units within the organisation, and (b) *external devolution*, where operations are devolved to agencies outside the organisation altogether (contracting-out). The twin aims in each instance are:

- The empowerment of local managers. Line managers have an incentive to make good use of resources; savings made under one budget head can be redeployed for other purposes. Instead of simply bidding for and allocating resources, the manager becomes a manager of resources. The units to which responsibility is devolved have more power and freedom to make executive decisions on a day-to-day basis.

- The facilitation of centralised direction and control. Managers must account for their increased freedoms. What is important is what is done with the resources and not simply ensuring that procedural rules are being followed. The centre can concentrate more on results and direction-giving, rather than being caught up in day-to-day minutiae.

The move to devolution is seen as operating at two levels. At the macro-level, there is devolution from the Department of Finance to line departments, as illustrated by the administrative budgets initiative. The intention is to continue this trend. Currently, departments have limited discretion and little incentive to control public expenditure. Yet if they are to be increasingly responsible for the delivery of outputs, they will need some discretion in the use of resources. This must be done in the context of a macro-control and audit framework. Such a macro-control framework is more likely to be effective than a detailed reliance on rules and policing by the centre, which can lead to situations where organisations are simultaneously over-controlled and out of control, because the detailed procedures become too complex and fail to operate effectively.

At a departmental level, there is a similar need for devolution from the centre to line managers, who are closest to the client system and dealing with clients on a day-to-day basis. This in turn will lead to changing relationships in departments. For example, staff in sections such as finance and personnel have an increasing support and advisory role in devolved management structures, as opposed to an authorisation and 'hands-on' role in the traditional hierarchical model.

3.4 Greater emphasis on managing for performance

The NESC Report *A strategy for the nineties* emphasises the need for enhancing the efficiency and effectiveness of government departments and the public service generally. The health strategy stresses the need for the Department of Health to be able to monitor and evaluate service and financial performance against national objectives and standards. Under his value for money investigations, the Comptroller and Auditor General will be looking at the adequacy of management systems in government departments for monitoring performance.

Performance management is central to the current agenda of public service management improvements. It is also inextricably tied in with devolution. The centre must be clear about the kind of results it is looking for from operational managers and develop appropriate monitoring and evaluation procedures. At the operational level, units and agencies must have clear targets for achievement, and structures and processes in place to enable the achievement of goals. In all, a new look is to be taken at performance and how it is managed in the public service.

Yet defining objectives and targets and measuring performance in the civil service is fraught with difficulties. The three 'E's – economy, efficiency and effectiveness – are used as guides when defining performance but they have limitations. Also, to allow people to innovate and develop, some time is needed that is not target driven. A balance is needed between too great a focus on performance and a limited focus on probity and due process.

Perhaps the biggest challenge facing departments is for them to become more output-oriented. This involves identifying and specifying the outputs they produce. For some activities, such as routine executive functions, this process may not be too difficult. But for many areas, such as policy advice and research, there are problems to overcome.

The biggest issue with regard to performance management is, perhaps, a behavioural one. To those opposed to the results-oriented approach, performance management is likely to be seen as at best an irrelevance and at worst an attempt to impose controls on behaviour in an autocratic manner. To supporters, performance management provides an opportunity to reflect on performance, learn from the best, and enhance service to the public. Performance management is as much about creating an appropriate culture as it is a technical process.

3.5 Emphasising quality of service to clients and citizens

Quality of service is mentioned as one of the key principles underpinning the health strategy. The education green paper also places great stress on quality, in particular the development of quality assurance in educational institutions. Civil service departments generally are giving increasing attention to quality of service issues.[28] The strategic management initiative identifies the issue of providing an excellent service to the public as one of the main items to be addressed at a strategic level in departments.

A recent analysis indicates several key aspects which should characterise the quality of interaction between departments and their clients:

- *Meeting clients' needs.* This includes searching out and identifying clients' needs, to ensure that actual needs are being met rather than perceived needs. It also involves separating out the various 'clients' with their different demands. A needs-based focus includes developing a sound knowledge of the various techniques available to determine needs, and the strengths and weaknesses of each.

- *Accessibility of the system to the client.* Accessibility includes physical accessibility in terms of ensuring the appropriate location and timing of services. Moves to regionalisation of services can be seen as one means of becoming more locally responsive. Accessibility also includes ensuring that the service is understandable to clients, through good form design, helpful systems and procedures and so on.

- *Client participation.* The purpose and focus of participation may vary significantly. Giving out information to clients, developing consultative and feed-back mechanisms, user forums, including clients on management committees – these mechanisms represent varying degrees of participation from fairly low-level to power-sharing arrangements.

- *Client redress.* The concept of quality of service includes the principle of redress when a client is treated badly. Procedures and practices to enable the issue of redress to be tackled equitably need to be established.

- *Client rights.* There are certain rights that clients have in relation to public services, derived from legal sources, the payment of taxes and basic democratic rights. These include the right to be informed, to a fair hearing, to be listened to, and to receive explanation. Increasingly, such rights are being gathered together in formal statements identifying categories of clients and specific performance standards.[29]

Another key feature of quality of service in the public sector is that quality is often seen as the preserve of professional staff providing a service e.g. doctors, teachers. In these circumstances, the role of management is often not to run quality procedures, but to ensure that quality management procedures and practices are put in place. Managers may use a range of incentives or sanctions to ensure that quality is on the agenda, leaving the professionals to design and run the system.

3.6 Getting things done through other organisations

If departments follow the path laid down for them in the recent government initiatives and reviews, they will increasingly concentrate on their strategic and policy formulation roles. Day-to-day management of activities is to be devolved to other units. Some of these units may be under fairly direct control of departments, such as the health authorities. In other instances the bodies responsible for getting things done may not be directly influenced by departments, for instance, voluntary bodies. In all cases, however, departmental management will be responsible for co-ordinating activities which range across a spread of organisations, to ensure that there is a consistency of approach to the implementation of government determined strategies.

Departments also have to manage international relationships and partnerships, such as the European Union, Here, the aim is to manage the relationship in such a way that Irish interests are placed on the policy agenda, and secured where possible.

In situations where there is some degree of 'control' relationship between a department and an agency, it is likely that some kind of formal or informal agreement will aim to determine the boundaries of the relationship. Increasingly, 'management by contract' rather than 'management by command' is seen as the catchphrase for how control is realised in such situations.

In situations where the control relationship is less direct between a department and various agencies, or where a department is liaising as a co-equal on the international front, it is the capacity to influence which is central to a department's ability to ensure co-operation and co-ordination. Establishing and building networks of organisations to achieve common aims is a major challenge for departments.

3.7 A move from procedural accountability to accountability for results

The C&AG (Amendment) Act 1993 can be seen as part of a move to shift the focus of public accountability. Traditionally, the interest in accountability has been on ensuring that public money is spent on the purposes and activities for which it is allocated. Increasingly, however, there is a move to include the concept of accountability for what has been achieved with the money which was spent. Value for money auditing has a results-oriented remit. The health strategy further extends the concept of accountability. Traditional accountability is through the minister and Oireachtas to the public. The health strategy raises the issue of decision-makers also being directly accountable to the consumers of the services.

These changes in accountability requirements mean that managers will (a) increasingly have to focus on the results achieved with the resources under their control, and (b) demonstrate these results to their clients, both in the Oireachtas and directly to the public. Whilst probity and procedural correctness will remain as key issues for accountability, they will be joined by an interest in cost-effective outcomes. Under such an accountability regime, the emphasis will be on:

- knowing what you are supposed to achieve
- knowing in a timely manner the results that have been achieved
- being able to demonstrate credibly what was achieved
- constantly striving for more cost-effective ways of achieving the results
- being able to show that you acted wisely on this knowledge i.e., that the decisions and actions taken were responsible in the light of what happened.[30]

To enable such a system to operate, evaluation practices and procedures will need to be integrated into programme management. Evaluation can underpin the accountability process, by providing the link between what has been and is being done, and what should be done.

4
Identifying the key roles of civil servants

4.1 Introduction

If civil servants are to meet the challenges arising from the changing environment in which they operate, they will need to develop new skills and capacities and enhance existing ones. But how do we establish what these skills and capacities are? Work is going on in the civil service to tackle the question. Many departments are currently undertaking training needs analyses and working through the implications of these analyses for skills and capacity development. The Civil Service Commission has recently completed a study of competencies needed at assistant principal officer level in the civil service.[31] In this chapter, the aim is to provide a context for this continuing work, by identifying the key roles which civil servants must take on if the issues identified in Chapters 2 and 3 are to be tackled effectively.[32] The skills and capacities needed to fulfil each role can then be identified and developed. Eight key roles are identified and explored for civil servants: strategist; policy analyst; broker; people manager; information manager; finance manager; monitor/evaluator; and change agent.

4.2 The civil servant as strategist

Strategy making is a complex issue in the civil service, particularly in defining the respective roles of politicians and civil servants. It is clear however, particularly from the strategic management initiative, that civil servants have a major role to play in developing strategic thinking and processes in the civil service.

The role of the civil servant as strategist is not simply that of a strategic planner. Strategic planning may take place where an organisation can control its environment, predict its course, or assume its stability.[33] There are many instances in the civil service where none of these conditions apply. In this context, the task of the civil servant is to stimulate strategic thinking and operationalise strategic processes rather than to plan.

In order to fulfil this strategist role, the civil servant will need to be able:

- *To scan the environment* for emerging issues, based on an understanding of the strengths and weaknesses of the department and the opportunities or threats facing it. This requires an understanding of changes in the environment, political values and organisational capacity.

- *To select and prioritise options* thrown up by the scanning process. This entails carrying out analyses of specific issues which are likely to be influential to the future running of the department. The strategic analysis envisaged here concerns the analysis of both 'hard' and 'soft' data so as to facilitate decision-making on emerging strategies. Needs assessment is a vital element of this analysis function.

- *To secure the benefits* from developed strategies, and ensure that they are realised. Communicating the strategy and ensuring that there is a shared vision of what is to be achieved, and how, is essential here, as is the ability to adapt organisational structures and processes to match the desired strategies.

4.3 The civil servant as policy analyst

Policy is a traditional aspect of a civil servant's job. Yet policy analysis is an area of work which is seen to be in need of enhancement. It has been said at times that civil servants have very good destructive analytical skills – the ability to break down and highlight the weaknesses in a case – but that the more constructive analytical skills are weak in comparison.

Policy analysis requires a mix of quantitative and qualitative skills. Quantitative methods are useful in order to help define and delimit issues and problems and to subject policy fields to rigorous scrutiny. But there are many policy issues where analysis using quantitative tools alone is inappropriate or unrealistic. There is also a need for policy analysts to have a range of qualitative methods and skills when dealing with complex public issues. Many different interests have to be consulted, and conflicting points of view identified and reconciled where possible.

Policy analysts must have a sound knowledge of the policy process, both in theory and practice. This will inform their ability to ask the right questions and determine the most appropriate methods for analysis. Analytical skills are needed to sift through the multiplicity of data that is available, and identify significant patterns and key variables.

4.4 The civil servant as broker

The 'brokerage' role for the civil servant arises from the fact that much of the work of civil servants involves getting things done through other organisations. In these circumstances, managers have to operate across rather than within organisations. They have to determine and develop their own organisation's role in a network of organisations involved in similar activities. In some of these networks, such as the provision of education or health services, the civil servant is concerned to ensure that the department takes a lead role. In other networks, such as the EU, the emphasis is on developing collaborative strategies and ensuring that ministerial interests are articulated and progressed.

Where the department takes the lead role, and has some control over the delivery agencies, civil servants will be expected to formalise arrangements by means of various types of contractual agreement. Contracting in these circumstances requires civil servants to be able to:

- Develop a 'mission' for collaborative enterprise and the translation of that mission into clearly specified aims and objectives to provide a focus for activities, including the design of agreements.

- Determine the type of contract most suitable to a particular situation. Contracts can range from 'hard' contracts which are highly legalistic and with detailed specifications of desired performance to 'soft' contracts where performance specification is more flexible and the agreement is more likely to be a collaborative effort between the various partners involved.

- Determine how best to monitor the contractor's performance. The type of reporting required e.g. annual reports, quarterly financial returns and the number and format of meetings between the partners, must be decided.

- Determine penalties for inadequate performance and rewards for good performance.

Where the department is operating in a collaborative or competitive manner as part of a network of organisations, without a direct control relationship, there will be a need for a different approach to secure particular interests. In these circumstances civil servants must have:

- An ability to understand and appreciate the viewpoint of other organisations, their culture and language.

- A knowledge of the resources available for influence, for instance financial, organisational and information skills.

- A clear sense of direction so that opportunities for influence can be taken pro-actively rather than followed re-actively.

4.5 The civil servant as people manager

It is often said that people are the most important resource of the civil service. Staff account for approximately 70 per cent of the running costs of departments. Clearly, how well staff are managed affects the performance of the civil service. Yet people management issues have not been seen to be well handled:

> The group consider that the major obstacle to significant public sector reform in Ireland is the outdated attitude to 'people' issues and inappropriate structures and systems governing human resource management.[34]

The traditional hierarchical structure in the civil service militates against good people management. Staff in senior positions may see their role in terms of their particular specialist function such as policy advice, rather than as the manager of a group of people.

Staff issues such as induction and development are seen as issues to be handed over to the personnel section. This can lead to a 'chicken and egg' situation where the personnel section are so busy dealing with detailed issues that they cannot make time to provide the support services to line managers to enable them to take on a more effective people management role.

If devolution of responsibilities is to take place and operate effectively, line managers must be equipped to take on the people management aspect of their job.

Team building and leadership is one particular area for development. Many civil service departments are increasingly emphasising team-based working as an effective approach to breaking down hierarchies and administrative/professional divides. This brings challenges both (a) for senior managers in establishing the teams and overcoming initial problems such as role definition, reporting relationships and rewards, and (b) for the team leaders, in how they handle the team members, chair meetings and committees and so on.

Similarly, promoting good performance and tackling the issue of underperformance is a key task for line managers. This issue is closely tied to performance appraisal. It is only in the context of agreement on specific targets and results to be achieved that an evaluation can be made of good or poor performance. Line managers must be able to specify and identify appropriate performance criteria and know the necessary and appropriate actions to take when these criteria are not met.

Communications also has a central part to play in good people management. Being able to manage two-way communication – informing staff of issues, strategies and goals and being open to feedback from staff – influences the level of performance achieved.

In order to perform effectively in the people management role, therefore, the civil servant will need:

- To develop human resource management capacities to complement position-specific skills.

- To encourage, lead and develop team-based working for many of the activities which traditionally have been carried out through the hierarchical structure.

- To emphasise communication, feedback and review. The ability to involve and inform staff, to increase knowledge of desired performance and clarify responsibility are important activities here.

- To facilitate staff appraisal and development. It is necessary to appraise staff in the context of departmental needs. The appraisal process needs to be used to develop staff, matching the needs of the individual and the department.

4.6 The civil servant as information manager

There are two elements to the role of information manager: the management of information technology (IT), and the management of information arising from IT and other sources.

The proper management of IT has the potential to facilitate organisational restructuring and to enable new ways of working to be operationalised. IT can change working relationships in departments, between departments, and between departments and their clients. But the extent to which it does so depends upon how the introduction and development of IT is managed. IT specialists, at a senior level, need to develop a range of consultancy and change management skills, as well as leadership skills, if the potential of IT as an enabler of organisational and structural change is to be realised. Similarly, IT expertise needs to be developed amongst line managers so they can communicate with specialists. These latter skills are as much if not more to do with managing and overseeing change enabled by technological developments, as they are to do with 'hands-on' experience with IT.

With regard to the management of information arising from IT and other sources, there is a need for civil servants to identify, gather, analyse and apply information to achieve the goals of the department. The requirement here is for a range of sources of information to be established; patterns, interrelationships and trends in the information to be identified and analysed; and solutions developed with supporting arguments where appropriate.

In summary then, the requirements on a civil servant to effectively fulfil the role of information manager are:

- To recognise the capability of IT to facilitate change in the civil service, through its contribution to competitiveness and the ability to change organisational structures and procedures.

- To develop a framework for information management in and across departments, recognising information as a major resource in government. In particular, there is a need to develop prior appraisal of IT investment strategies so that the full range of IT benefits can be specified and subsequently assessed.

- To enhance analytical capabilities (policy analysis, financial analysis and so on), so that full value is derived from the improved management information arising from IT.

4.7 The civil servant as financial manager

Devolution of financial management responsibility to departments, and to line managers in departments, as exemplified by the administrative budgets initiative and commitments in the current policy agreement *A government of renewal*, leads to changes in the financial managerial role of civil servants. This is particularly the case for senior managers, line managers and managers of budget sub-heads.

For senior managers, the move is a shift from one of overseeing the delivery of service to a more strategic role, responsible for setting overall financial direction and priorities, linking resource costs to results.

For line managers, the shift is towards a more pro-active managerial approach regarding the use of financial resources. On the budgeting front, line managers have responsibility for ensuring that budgets are related to output measures and indicators.

For budget sub-head holders, the change which devolution brings is from the authorisation of expenditure under their control towards taking a more advisory stance, with increased initiative being given to line managers regarding decisions on the application of financial resources.

Devolution is also closely linked to, and has implications for, financial planning and control generally. In this context, the recent changes in government accounting procedures and emphasis on asset management are important. If the move from a cash-based towards a more accrual-based accounting system continues, this will facilitate accountability and the move to a more output-based, results-oriented system of financial management.

In summary, the move to devolution impacts on the control and use of financial resources by civil servants. In particular:

- The focus is switched away from the traditional emphasis on input control and probity, towards a more managerial model emphasising performance and, in particular, whether the required outputs are produced for a given allocation of financial resources.

- Negotiating and agreeing budgets becomes a key managerial task, requiring planning capabilities and liaison with resource allocation bodies, both internal and external to the department.

- Systems must be developed to enable the tracking of financial information and to facilitate the active management of budgets, particularly with regard to variances from planned expenditure.

4.8 The civil servant as monitor/evaluator

The role of the civil servant as monitor/evaluator is largely a function of the relationship between the political and administrative systems. If departments are judged on staying within their voted expenditure, this is what will count. If ministers demand client-oriented results, this will work its way down through the system. As mentioned in the previous chapter, there is an increasing interest in, and focus on, accountability for results and performance management. These imperatives are influencing the type of monitoring and evaluation that is expected of civil servants.

Results are central to performance management. Yet civil servants often face difficulties in specifying results and knowing when they are doing well. Because there are multiple constituencies which departments must serve, the specification of goals can be problematic. Managers need to attempt to set out clearly the various constituencies or stakeholders to be affected by the performance of the department, ask what results are most relevant to them, and establish trade-offs and priorities. Targets with a results focus also need to be set. Managers must be able to set challenging yet realistic targets for tasks, and agree them with superiors and subordinates.

Managers then need to bring others in the division along with them. Team review meetings held by managers can play a particularly important role in any monitoring process. The topics for discussion at such meetings will vary depending on the level in the department affected: at the 'shop floor' level, meetings are likely to focus on progress on operational issues and problems. Further up the management structure, meetings concentrate more on performance trends, policy and direction and a 'brokerage' role where operational targets are in conflict. Involving front-line staff in the process is a crucial aspect of this element of performance management. Front line staff are often the ones most aware of the successes and failures of the organisation, and they need to be seen as participants in the monitoring process, not just the recipients and implementors of instructions.

Performance monitoring systems and processes also need to be closely linked to staff appraisal and development.

Monitoring also needs to be complemented by programme evaluation. Evaluation is concerned with the basic questions about a programme: is it worth running; what is its impact. Sometimes, such evaluation activities are carried out by civil servants themselves. Other times, civil servants may commission outside experts to conduct evaluation studies on their behalf.

The main implications of the monitoring/evaluation role for civil servants are:

- A focus on results. The specification of goals and targets and the question of results for whom, what kind of results and how many results all must be addressed.

- Involvement of superiors and subordinates in the results-setting and monitoring process.

- The ability to demonstrate the results achieved to interested audiences in a manner which engages their attention and encourages reflection.

- A requirement for evaluation capabilities to enable judgments to be made on the continuing relevance of particular programmes and activities. These capabilities may include both those needed to commission an evaluation study, and those needed to carry out evaluations.

4.9 The civil servant as change agent

The proposed changes in civil service management practice outlined in Chapters 2 and 3 require a change in the culture of the civil service. In particular, there is a need for innovation. Making new policies work effectively in practice, rather than simply developing policies, is crucial if the practical problems that arise when putting policies into effect are to be overcome.[35]

Civil servants must be able to draw up effective change management strategies, in consultation with staff and implement those strategies through them. They must also be able to lead change for the sector for which they have responsibility. Simply willing people to do things differently does not work.

To facilitate such change requires skills and capacities that are different from those needed to manage settled and routine tasks and programmes. In particular, there is a need for civil servants to be able to:

- Develop a vision of the proposed change process, based on the plans and priorities of the government and aimed at addressing current deficiencies in practice or culture.

- Anticipate and assess the impact of change, including: an assessment of the availability and suitability of the resources required for change; and the ability to recognise and plan to overcome resistance to change.

- Communicate an understanding of what change is occurring, and how and why it is occurring. This process also involves creating an environment conducive to change.

- Lead others in adapting to the requirements of change.

4.10 Summary

The roles which have been outlined here, and the consequent skills and capacities needed of civil servants to fulfil these roles, are not mutually exclusive. There are significant areas of overlap. For example, developing a vision to manage the change process is clearly linked to the strategic management role. Team meetings to review progress as a monitor/evaluator involves people management skills. The purpose here is not to arrive at exclusive categories, but to identify certain thematic roles that civil servants can be expected to perform in the light of current and likely future changes in civil service management practice. These roles, and the associated skills and capacities required if the roles are to be performed effectively, set a framework for the future development of civil servants.

One of the central messages coming across from this exploration of roles is the shift in emphasis from the civil servant as administrator to the civil servant as manager.[36] This trend, also evident internationally, highlights the need for the development of managerial skills and capacities. It is also evident that this increasing emphasis on management is done within the context of a 'results' focus to the work of civil servants. More attention is to be given to the explicit definition of the outputs and outcomes of civil service activity.

A further point concerning the skills and capacities identified here is that they are general in nature, as opposed to being position-specific. They apply across the civil service, rather than being confined to one specific area of relevance. Naturally, there is also a need for the development of position-specific skills and capacities. For example, civil servants dealing with foreign trade issues may need particular language skills and negotiating capabilities. In certain sections, particular legal expertise may be required. The identification of these position-specific skills and capacities is beyond the scope of this report. But their identification and development is an important issue for the civil service, and one to be tackled through the departmental training needs anlaysis process. Also, as the skills and capacities outlined here are general in nature, it is difficult to be specific as to which are most relevant to particular levels (senior managers, middle managers and so on) or divisions (client delivery sections, policy advice sections, finance sections and so on). Two general guidelines are proposed as to how this issue can be tackled:

(a) In the light of their strategic management analyses carried out as part of the strategic management initiative, departments should be in a position where they have a vision of the future strategy for the organisation. The requisite skills and capacities to bring about this desired future can be determined, using the above roles as a framework for this task. The particular locations or levels of management where new skills and capacity development is particularly needed could be identified through this process.

(b) The Civil Service Commission have recently completed a study of the competencies needed at assistant principal level in the civil service. This is the beginning of a process to define competencies for particular grades. This ongoing work can draw on the findings of this study, setting out in detail the competencies needed at each grade level to fulfil particular roles.

5
Towards a curriculum for management education and development for the Irish civil service

5.1 Introduction

So far, this study has investigated some important features of developments in the civil service in Ireland, and their implications for civil servants in terms of skills and capacity development. The study has identified the increasing emphasis which is being placed on managerial skills and capacities. This raises significant questions for management education and development. The next two chapters give pointers to what needs to be done to enhance skills and capacity development. In this chapter the base on which a curriculum for management education and development in the Irish civil service can be founded is set down. In particular, two issues are investigated. First, the need for an appropriate model to establish the knowledge base for management education is explored. The aim here is to set out the basic parameters within which a curriculum for management education for civil servants should operate. The focus is on the longer-term, educational needs of civil servants. Secondly, the topics which should inform both management education and development initiatives are outlined. These topics outline the core skills and capacities needed by civil servants. The following chapter then goes on to identify how this core curriculum can be adapted and applied in practice in the changing environment within which civil service management is operating.

5.2 An appropriate model for the knowledge base of management education in the civil service

In determining how civil servants should be developed for their roles, the knowledge base of management education needs to be clarified. Some commentators propose that essentially, management tasks are similar in the public and private sectors and, therefore, generic (often private sector dominated) management programmes are appropriate. In this scenario, a generic model of management is put forward as the most appropriate base for management education. The public and private sectors are seen as converging, sharing common problems and solutions. The complex interactions between public and private firms mean that their needs are inter-twined.

Others stress that the political dimension is a defining characteristic of the public service, and that programmes need to be specifically targeted at the particular needs of public service management.[37] In this model, management education is based on the premise that managers need to be informed of the distinctive nature of public administration. The focus is on those aspects which are deemed to be particular to public administration, such as the policy and political process.

The proposition put forward here is that, whilst many tasks are similar in both the public and private sectors, the environment within which tasks in the civil service take place means that there are particular complexities and constraints acting on managers operating in the civil service. Issues such as political accountability, a requirement for equity in decision-making, and serving citizens rather than customers, all serve to illustrate that managing in the civil service requires management education support which is particularly targeted at the needs of the civil servant.[38]

Yet management education for civil servants must not be confined to what might be termed the 'traditional' model of public administration, with an emphasis on politics and policy analysis. Whilst such issues remain central to management in the civil service, they are only a part of what is needed. In particular, the findings from this study indicate that the world of the civil servant has changed significantly in recent years. New pressures and priorities are arising which influence how civil servants fulfil their duties. There is an increasing emphasis on a more managerial approach and on service to the citizen.

How can the demands being placed on civil servants be encapsulated so as to provide a sound knowledge base for management education support? One means is to make use of the domain model of human services organisations, which has been used in the UK in recent years to illustrate the distinctive nature of public service management.[39]

In the domain model, each human service organisation comprises multiple systems, divided into three domains, each with its own set of governing principles, success measures, structural arrangement and work modes. The three domains are:

- *The policy domain.* Where policies for action are formulated and developed by appointed or elected members.

- *The management domain.* Where cost-effectiveness and efficiency issues dominate.

- *The service domain.* Where professional expertise is the dominant factor, operating under self-governing arrangements.

Figure 3 illustrates the three domains and their distinguishing characteristics.

The presence of three domains in the same organisation has implications for the management of those organisations. The argument behind the theory is that each domain is in a permanent state of potential conflict with the other domains, as each attempts to assert its predominance. These tensions must be managed. Also, civil servants must operate within and between all three domains. So, for example, senior managers operating at the policy domain/management domain interface may need to employ particular skills associated with their strategic role, such as

FIGURE 3 — The domains of public service organisations and their characteristics

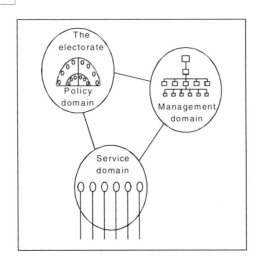

	Policy domain	**Management domain**	**Service domain**
Principles	Consent of the governed	Hierarchical control and co-ordination	Automony Self-regulation
Success measures	Equity	Cost efficiency Effectiveness	Quality of service Good standards of practice
Structure	Representative Participative	Bureaucratic	Collegial
Work models	Voting Bargaining Negotiating	Use of linear techniques and tools	Client-specific, Problem-solving

Source: Adapted from Talbot, op. cit.

working through the policy implications of changes in political priorities. Middle managers operating at the management domain/service domain interface may need to apply skills associated with their brokerage and people management roles, such as communicating policies and encouraging changes in professional practice.

Thus, from a management education viewpoint, managers in the civil service need a sound knowledge of each of the domains - how they operate, and the implications for managerial practice and behaviour. Each domain has its own particular fields of knowledge associated with it, which acts as the basis for understanding of the domain:

- Policy domain: politics, government, the legal system

- Management domain: management, economics

- Service domain: social policy and administration, sociology

One problem is that these fields of knowledge can easily fail to work together, as they reflect differing academic and institutional disciplines and divisions. As one commentator has noted: 'The fields of politics and government, social policy and sociology, and business and management have remained divided, usually in separate faculties or departments, and often jealously guarding their territories. Instead of the respective experts providing a rich synergy from their differing perspectives all too often there has simply been mutual incomprehension'.[40]

A crucial challenge, therefore, in the establishment of a knowledge base for management education for civil servants is:

(a) to ensure that civil servants have a solid grounding in the fields of knowledge associated with the policy, management and service domains, and

(b) to ensure that these fields of knowledge are provided in an integrated and linked manner, so as to develop a fully rounded picture of the environment in which the civil servant operates.

5.3 Topics for inclusion in a management education and development curriculum

A knowledge base for management education in the civil service has been outlined, with the main broad fields of knowledge of relevance to civil service management identified. A next step is to identify the main topics that would inform a management education and development curriculum, establishing the skills and capacities needed to complement the knowledge base.

Table 2 outlines twelve topics that are central to the development of managers in the civil service. The topics are derived from information obtained from interviews with senior civil servants, and from an analysis of the themes guiding civil service development and the associated roles of civil servants outlined in Chapters 3 and 4. The topics outlined cannot all be neatly classified by the domain or role with which they are associated. Nevertheless, they provide an outline of the kind of issues to be covered if civil servants are to fulfil the roles expected of them and to operate in the policy, management and/or service domains.

The priority to be given to these topics crucially depends upon the context within which civil service departments are operating. At the present time, the move to strategic management in the Irish civil service is a primary driving force for skills and capacity development. Particular stress therefore needs to be placed on the skills needed to operate strategically in the provision of public services.

The first five topics mentioned - strategic management, policy analysis and evaluation, organisational analysis and design, managing for results, and improving service delivery to the citizen

TABLE 2

Topics for inclusion in a management education and development curriculum*

Topics primarily associated with managing strategically
Strategic management. Includes: – scanning the environment for trends, opportunities and threats – agenda setting – determining and appraising options
Policy analysis and evaluation. Includes: – developing and critically using a range of sources of information – establishing patterns and trends from data investigation – integrating evaluation with the decision-making process
Organisational analysis and design. Includes: – selecting appropriate structures and processes – devolving responsibility and delegating tasks – recognising the key role of informal systems and networks
Managing for results. Includes: – setting objectives and targets for multiple constituencies – developing performance review and appraisal systems – creating a results-oriented culture
Improving service delivery to the citizen. Includes: – determining the role of the citizen: consumer, client, partner – setting quality standards and targets – assessing citizen's needs and wants

Table 2 continued

Topics primarily associated with managing resources
Managing people. Includes: – leading and motivating – staff selection, deployment and development – communicating and negotiating
Managing information technology. Includes: – managing IT to facilitate organisational restructuring – developing IT expertise – prior appraisal and evaluation of IT investment
Expenditure planning and control. Includes: – budgeting and budgetary control – activity planning; linking outputs to resources – managing variances
Public accountability. Includes: – establishing value-for-money concepts and initiatives – demonstrating what has been achieved in a clear and accessible manner – clarifying the specifics of delegation of authority and responsibility

Table 2 continued

Topics primarily associated with managing working relationships
Working with ministers/Oireachtas. Includes: – liaising with ministers – reporting to the Dáil and Dáil committees – answering parliamentary questions and representations
Managing relationships with external agencies. Includes: – management by contract – managing relationships with the EU – building networks
Re-active policy advice/decision-making. Includes: – responding to threats and opportunities – coping with tight deadlines – learning lessons from past crises

* This table is adapted from a similar table in Lewis Gunn, 'Public management: a third approach', *Public Money and Management*, Spring/Summer, 1988, pp. 21-25.

– are all concerned with issues of central concern to the strategic management process. Strategic management is an obvious topic in its own right, being concerned with the formulation, implementation and evaluation of strategy. Policy analysis and evaluation provides a context for strategy making. By understanding policies and their impact the civil servant keeps in tune with the policy environment within which strategies take shape. Organisational analysis and design refers to a key issue in strategic management: establishing whether or not the organisation has the structures and processes, capabilities and capacities needed to see through the strategies determined upon. Managing for results reflects the issues which arise when focusing on the implementation of strategic management; translating broad strategies to objectives and targets for divisions and units and developing associated performance management systems in order to monitor and manage the intended outputs and outcomes. Improving service delivery to the citizen is a topic highlighted in the strategic management initiative and is concerned with managing the quality of service provision from the perspective of the citizen. Needs identification and specification is a key requirement here.

The next four topics listed – managing people, managing information technology, expenditure planning and control, and public accountability – refer to resource management in its broadest sense. Managing people is a key requirement and a recognition of the fact that results and service delivery come through the people in the organisation. Managers must be able to manage both the 'hard' techniques such as manpower planning, and also the 'softer' behavioural skills needed to influence and motivate staff. Managing information technology involves recognising the potential role of IT in facilitating new patterns of service provision and organisational structuring. Expenditure planning and control is a topic focused on the development of budgetary and associated skills at management level in the civil service. Business and activity planning at divisional and unit level is a key element in this area. Public accountability refers to the stewardship role played by managers in ensuring probity and value for money from the wide range of resources that the civil service brings to bear in overseeing and providing public services.

The final three topics included in the table – working with ministers/Oireachtas, managing relationships with external agencies, and re-active policy advice/decision-making – refer to the multiplicity of relationships which civil servants must manage in the course of their duties. Working with ministers and the Oireachtas is obviously a key dimension of a managers's job in the civil service and a topic which any curriculum for management education and development must include. Understanding and working with and through the political process is central to effective performance in the civil service. Managing relationships with external agencies is a major and growing task for many civil servants. It includes the need for enhanced knowledge of managing relationships internationally, particularly with the EU. It also refers to the need to manage relationships with executive, voluntary and other agencies which fall under a department's aegis, in the context of changing practices in how these relationships operate. Re-active policy advice/decision-making as a topic reflects the realities of civil service management where much of the work which arises is a response to external stimuli which acquire importance in the political process. Knowing how to manage such activities in the most effective and timely manner is an important skill requirement for civil servants.

The extent to which these twelve topics are best covered by management education programmes, development programmes, or a mixture of both, depends upon the particular skills under scrutiny and the needs of the organisation. Some skills, particularly those with a 'harder' focus such as policy analysis and budgeting, are well suited to being tackled through management education. Other skills, particularly the 'softer' skills such as motivation, influencing and communications, are better catered for through management development, with an emphasis on learning from experience.

It should also be noted that these topics represent the perceived needs for a curriculum at a particular point in time. The needs and context obviously change over time. There is an associated requirement to periodically review, evaluate and revise any outline of topics such as the ones indicated here, to ensure that they continue to meet the needs of civil servants. The development of a curriculum for management education and development is a continuing and evolutionary process.

5.4 Conclusions

Through the use of the domain theory model and the selection of key topics, a knowledge and skills base for a curriculum for management education and development in the civil service has been outlined. This base is derived from an analysis of the needs of civil servants, the changing trends in civil service management practice, and the roles which civil servants are expected to discharge.

The base for the curriculum is not intended to promote a standardisation of approach to management education and development. Some managers might have a need for development in one area, such as the policy domain, and not in the other domains. For other managers, the most appropriate approach might be further development in particular specialist areas, such as health or education management. There will be circumstances where a generic management programme involving a mix of private and public sector practitioners is the most relevant and appropriate means of meeting particular development needs. The role of the base outlined here is to provide a context for management education and development, to meet the needs of the Irish civil service. The main fields of knowledge and subject areas are identified and can be adapted and drawn from as appropriate. However, this curriculum for individual managerial learning will be of limited use unless it is set in the broader context of organisational learning. The benefits that arise from management education and development are only fully obtained if both the individual and the organisation get added-value from the intervention. The means by which this base curriculum can be applied to the dynamic and changing circumstances in which the Irish civil service now finds itself is discussed in the next chapter.

6
Developing a learning culture in the Irish civil service

6.1 Introduction

Having identified the skills and capacities required if civil servants are to manage effectively, it is necessary to determine the appropriate framework that will reinforce, maintain and enhance these skills and capacities. The task is how best to create and sustain a 'learning culture' in civil service departments and offices, such that there is a constant focus on, and commitment to learning. To create such a learning climate requires (a) processes to be put in place to ensure the generation, reinforcement and sustaining of organisational capacities, and (b) the creation of learning organisations in the civil service.

6.2 Setting the context – generating, reinforcing and sustaining capacities

The skills and capacities needed in the civil service derive both from a knowledge of past experience, and a future vision of what the civil service should be. The strategic management initiative is concerned with developing this future vision, looking not only at the work to be done, but also the structures, systems and processes that are required. At the level of the civil service as a whole, developing the organisational capacity to meet these requirements will necessitate six management practices being defined: selection and development to help generate capacities; appraisal and rewards to reinforce capacities; and organisation design and communication to sustain capacities.[41] Figure 4 sets out a framework for capacity development based on these six management practices.

The two management practices applied to the generation of capacities are selection and development. The selection process

FIGURE 4

A framework for capacity development

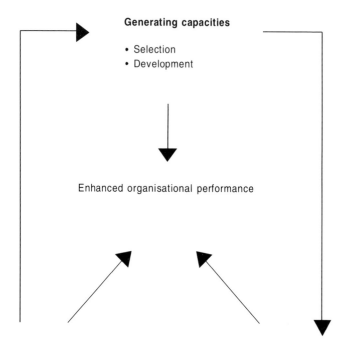

Source: Adapted from Ulrich and Lake, op. cit.

deals with the recruitment of staff into the civil service, the induction and probation of those staff, and the promotion of staff. Once inside the civil service, staff can develop new skills and capacities through training and other development activities. The need is to promote the development of individual learning that also matches the requirements of the organisation. Unless development takes place within the context of the future strategic needs of the organisation, it will fail to be fully effective.

Reinforcing capacities ensures that civil servants continually focus their attentions on the skills and capacities required, and behave in a manner consistent with those capacities. Two management practices are responsible for reinforcement: appraisal and rewards. Effective appraisal schemes require clarity of purpose, an organisational culture supportive of performance appraisal, and commitment on the part of management and staff.[42] In particular, distinguishing between appraisal for development and appraisal for reward is crucial, as is linking the appraisal system with broader departmental performance management systems, and setting clear, agreed output-oriented targets in this context. In general terms, rewards have an important role to play in encouraging desired attitudes and behaviours, and if used properly, in motivating staff to perform fully to their abilities. It is important to note that rewards are not just financial in nature. Personal and public recognition of a job well done can act as incentives. So too can increasing responsibility and giving more interesting and challenging projects to those who perform well. Moves to delegation of authority and removal of what are seen as trivial constraints can act as significant incentives and enhance the motivation of staff.

Once systems and procedures are in place to generate and reinforce the required skills and capacities in the civil service, the challenge then is to ensure that these skills and capacities evolve and persist over time. The two management practices that are used to help sustain capacities are organisational design and communication. Organisational design addresses questions such as what shape and structure an organisation should take; and how accountability and responsibility issues are to be tackled. Organisational design is important for sustaining capacities in the civil service, in that how departments are structured, the degree of delegation, the nature of reporting and control systems, all send out signals as to how civil servants should operate and behave. Communication processes include the various aspects of information flow within and between organisations. They help to sustain capacities by providing employees with information about the activities that are valued by the organisation. A key element in communication, and one which is seen to be missing to a large extent at present, is the ability to tell people when they are underperforming, and offer constructive criticism.

These management practices which need to be tackled if organisational capacities are to be generated, reinforced and sustained are issues which are being addressed at a service wide level across the civil service.[43] They provide the background context within which departments and offices must operate when progressing the task of developing and fostering a learning climate, wherein the skills and capacities identified in this research can be effectively applied so as to meet management and operational needs. These contextual management practices must be tackled, but they will not of themselves ensure the creation of a learning climate. This is a task which also requires the input of individual organisations.

6.3 Creating and sustaining a learning organisation

A process of change stimulated by the strategic management initiative and the government's reforms outlined in *A government of renewal* is taking place in civil service management practice. To adapt to this dynamic setting for skills and capacity development, individual departments and offices need to evolve a process for stimulating management development. It is suggested here that the concept of the learning organisation offers a framework for matching the needs arising from the change process to practical skills and capacity developments.

The intention here is not to suggest that departments and offices suddenly transform themselves into learning organisations. Rather, it is to suggest that they take steps to begin the process of putting learning at the heart of their activities, guiding skills and capacity development. Indeed, many departments and offices have started out on this process. The training needs analysis carried out under the aegis of the training initiative fund, and the processes put in place to implement the strategic management initiative, are necessary first steps in creating a culture which promotes skills and capacity development in the context of learning and organisational development.

In this section, the concept of the learning organisation is explored at three levels: definitions of the learning organisation; characteristics of a learning organisation; and guidelines as to how to develop a learning organisation.

Definitions of the learning organisation

The learning organisation is a concept which has gained increasing influence in the literature on management and organisation development in recent years.[44] However, no one definition of what a learning organisation is or looks like has gained credence. Some theorists indicate that generating new ways of thinking is what a learning organisation should be about. Others indicate that thinking on its own is not enough, and that behavioural changes are needed for organisational learning to take place.[45] A simple definition, yet one which captures the complexity of organisational learning is that a learning organisation is:

> an organisation which facilitates the learning of all its members and continuously transforms itself.[46]

This definition indicates that (a) individual learning is the focus; it is not enough simply to do a lot of training to be a learning organisation, and (b) learning only fully takes effect when there are accompanying changes in the way that an organisation arranges its work. Skills and capacity development is fostered by encouraging learning by individual members, allied with a continual process of organisational development.

Characteristics of a learning organisation

Having established some idea of what the term 'learning organisation' means, it is important to develop a picture of what a learning organisation might look like. This is not a simple task, as practice is likely to differ from organisation to organisation. There is no ideal blueprint for the learning organisation, as each organisation's own development needs and operating environment determines the approach to be adopted. However, having made this point, there are a number of characteristics that have been identified in the literature that seem to lie behind successful learning organisations:

- *Learning and working are synonymous.* Learning is not seen as an activity that lies in a particular 'province', such as the training division, separate from the mainstream activity of the organisation. Instead, the work activities which take place are viewed as learning opportunities. Successes and failures are reviewed, and lessons learnt from these experiences.

- *Individual members are encouraged to learn and to develop their potential.* This refers to the 'climate' which exists in the organisation. The creation of such an environment is a difficult challenge in a civil service setting where risk minimisation is often a central feature of the organisational culture. Support for employee initiative can be signalled by explicit reference in the organisation's strategy, by promoting team-based work focused on innovative tasks, and by senior management demonstrating to staff that new ideas will be encouraged and given serious consideration.

- *Systematic problem solving is encouraged.* A rigorous, analytical approach to problem solving is encouraged, rather than relying on assumptions and guesswork. Simple statistical tools such as cause and effect diagrams and pareto charts are used to provide and organise data from which inferences and solutions can be drawn.

- *The learning culture extends beyond the boundaries of the organisation.* This characteristic takes two forms:

    (a) The main stakeholders of the organisation (clients, customers, suppliers and so on) are actively encouraged to participate in the learning environment. They may be involved in workshops, task forces on specific issues, or join in particular training and development programmes.

    (b) Benchmarking is used to identify, learn from and emulate best practice in a particular field of activity. This involves a search to identify best practice organisations, study of practice and performance against identified best practice standards, and the development and implementation of recommendations.

    The concept of learning beyond organisation boundaries is a particularly important one for the civil service. Departments and offices share many common issues and problems, and many policy fields straddle several areas of responsibility.

- *Human resource development is a central element of the organisation's overall strategy.* Instead of being separated out as a largely industrial relations function, personnel management is seen as a major activity of the organisation. Individual and organisational learning are promoted as a core function which is taken seriously at a corporate level in the organisation.

- *The transfer of knowledge is promoted throughout the organisation.* This characteristic has two dimensions:

  (a) Effort is put into ensuring that ideas are spread broadly throughout the organisation, rather than concentrated in a few hands. The use of written and visual presentations, job rotation and so on is encouraged so as to ensure the spread of skills and capacities that have been learnt from particular activities.

  (b) Individual learning is used to make necessary changes to the assumptions, strategies, operating structures and processes of the organisation.[47]

In conclusion, the characteristics of a learning organisation would indicate that a conscious approach is needed on the part of departments and offices to skills acquisition, retention and enhancement. The learning organisation can be said to facilitate a cycle of learning related activities focused on skills and capacity development, as illustrated in Figure 5. Starting with strategy, this provides the backdrop and the vision of the future of the organisation that sets the context for organisational learning. Development needs analysis focuses on identifying and defining the main skills and capacity requirements that are needed in the organisation. The identification of learning opportunities facilitates a structured and systematic approach to skills and capacity enhancement, ensuring that appropriate opportunities are recognised and exploited.

The cycle does not necessarily need to follow a particular staged approach to its implementation. The cycle can be entered at any stage. Also, actions taken in one area can feed into the others. For instance, a development needs analysis may identify and promote particular new strategy developments which are emerging in an

A Learning Cycle Setting for Skills and Capacity Development in Organisations

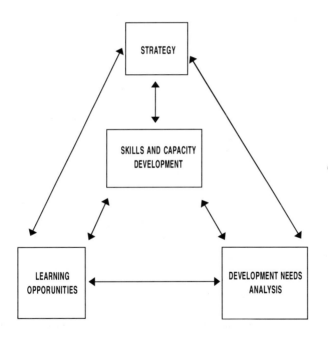

organisation. Learning opportunities may arise from the development of a particular strategy. The main point is that processes and structures are in place to consciously utilise such opportunities for skills and capacity development.

Guidelines for developing a learning organisation

Whilst there is a growing body of literature on guidelines as to how to facilitate organisational learning, little of this literature is drawn from public sector experience. One notable exception is the development of a model of organisational learning in a public service setting in Canada.[48] This research indicates a number of guidelines pertinent to civil service departments and offices which wish to foster and promote the learning organisation concept:

- *Identify and delimit the role of the organisation in promoting learning.* The emphasis must shift from the organisation providing specific, isolated training events towards the integration of formal and informal learning activities. The organisation should be seen as 'empowering' individual learning opportunities rather than providing development activities. In this scenario, the organisation supports and facilitates skills development and acquisition, providing a framework within which individuals take responsibility for their own learning. The development of training needs analyses by departments and offices provide an example of the organisation defining and delimiting its role.

- *Recognise the educative nature of the workplace.* The aim here is to be aware of the learning opportunities that exist in the course of day-to-day work activities in the organisation. For example, policy and strategy formulation can be structured as a learning process. Information systems can be used to assist learning and the questioning of current operational practices. Task teams set up to investigate specific topics can be given a developmental brief as well as the specific task in hand.

- *Implement a learner-centred approach to development.* Within the context of organisational objectives and needs, the focus is on the development of individual learning strategies, with primary responsibility for the development and implementation of the learning strategy resting with the learner him or herself. This will be through a mixture of formal training and development activities (such as courses, coaching, workshops) and informal activities (such as being given an unfamiliar task, learning from peers, subordinates and superiors).

- *Encourage active participation by management in employee development.* This is a recognition that learning is not simply the responsibility of the personnel division or a training section. Managers have a responsibility to ensure that the skills and capacities needed for their operations to run successfully are acquired and developed by employees working with them. The role of the manager is to help to define suitable learning opportunities relevant to the organisation needs, and to provide support to the employees in developing appropriate learning strategies. Managers may also be well placed to provide mentoring to employees.

- *Establish learning facilitators to aid individual development.* Both within and outside the organisation, individuals should be identified whose role it is to facilitate individual centred learning in its organisational setting. Their role is to help develop the framework for individual learning strategies and ensure that the organisation has a coherent view of skills and capacity development, and its role in organisational development.

- *Open up boundaries to ensure learning from others.* Within the organisation, this means using such activities as conferences, seminars and project teams to ensure a fresh flow of ideas and their cross-fertilisation. Linking to the external environment, it is important that employees with outside contacts act as scanners for the organisation, sharing information and ensuring that the external perspective is brought to bear in the learning process. The assistant secretary and principal officer networks provide examples of learning opportunities and which cross departmental boundaries.

These guidelines set a framework for the creation of a learning organisation:

> Adoption of a strategic approach to learning signals a move away from 'teaching' and towards a focus on the individual and the learning process. It reflects a recognition of the educative nature of work and the many ways in which individuals learn. It seeks to provide a framework for a dialogical approach to the identification of needs and objectives; the fostering of developmental partnership between managers and employees; and the integration of a broad range of learning experiences and events directly related to a defined learning aim developed by the learner and the organisation. The strategic approach presumes an organisational philosophy which values the individual, and supports individual development. The organisation must be prepared to relinquish control over individual development and focus on facilitating and integrating learning rather than regulating programmes and dictating participation.[49]

Table 3 indicates steps which are being taken in the Department of Transport, Energy and Communications to create a learning climate focused on issues concerned with strategic management in the department. It provides a practical example of the kind of steps to be taken in facilitating skills and capacity development in a strategic context.

TABLE 3

Creating a learning climate focused on strategic management issues in the Department of Transport, Energy and Communications*

- Regular off-site meetings of the Management Advisory Committee to discuss strategic management only.

- Meetings of (i) PO's and equivalents, (ii) AP's, (iii) HEO/AO's to discuss strategic management issues.

- Weekly Management Advisory Committee meetings with circulation of agenda to principal officers and equivalent grades.

- Establishment of standing committees (composed of principal officers and equivalent grades), covering:

    – personnel
    – training and development
    – finance
    – information technology.

- Establishment of organisation and development unit to undertake:

    – training needs analyses
    – comprehensive training and development programme for all grades with a focus on skills identified as required in the department

* Taken from presentation given by the department to accounting officers at Dublin Castle, 18 April 1994.

6.4 Conclusions

The aim here has been to set out what needs to happen for the skills and capacities identified elsewhere in this study to be institutionalised in the civil service. In effect, at a civil service-wide level it requires changing or evolving practices in selection and development, appraisal and rewards, and organisational design and communication. At the organisational level, it requires the development of a learning organisation philosophy and approach to individual development. This is not something that will happen overnight. The emphasis, as with the strategic management initiative, is on establishing an evolutionary process whereby these issues are tackled on an incremental, step-by-step basis.

Recent initiatives impacting on the civil service, such as information technology developments, administrative budgets and the strategic management initiative, provide the context within which skills and capacity development of civil servants takes place. The policy document *A government of renewal* proposes further significant change in the way the civil service operates and performs. In all, the structure, composition, tasks and processes of civil service management are under change.

In order to cope with this changing environment, civil servants need new skills and capacities. Referring back to Chapter 1 of this study, the demand is for the increasing professionalisation of public administration. This study is a contribution toward defining the parameters of this profession, defining the boundaries of the discipline, its content areas, and suggesting linkages between education and development and the creation and sustaining of a learning organisation. The study provides a framework for enhancing the various roles of the civil servant in a changing and turbulent environment.

REFERENCES

1. OECD, *Performance management in government*, Public management occasional paper No. 3, OECD: Paris, 1994.

2. Christopher Hood, 'A public management for all seasons?', *Public Administration*, Vol. 61, Spring, 1991, pp. 3-19.

3. These initiatives are explored in more detail in Chapter 2.

4. *A government of renewal*, a policy agreement between Fine Gael, the Labour Party and Democratic Left, 1994.

5. Interview in the *Irish Times*, 13 January 1995.

6. Desmond J. Kelly, 'Public administration in a mature democracy', *Administration*, Vol. 41, No. 1, 1993, pp. 72-79.

7. International trends in public service management, both in theory and practice, are explored in detail in a separately published report produced as a part of this study: Richard Boyle, *Towards a new public service*, Dublin: Institute of Public Administration, 1995.

8. National Economic and Social Council, *A strategy for the nineties: economic stability and structural change*, Report No. 89, Dublin: NESC, 1990.

9. National Economic and Social Council, *A strategy for competitiveness, growth and employment*, Report No. 96, Dublin: NESC, 1993.

10. Industrial Policy Review Group, *A time for change: industrial policy for the 1990s*, Dublin: Stationery Office, 1992.

11. *Charting our education future*, White Paper on Education, Dublin: Stationery Office, 1995.

12. Department of Health, *Shaping a healthier future: a strategy for effective healthcare in the 1990s*, Dublin: Stationery Office, 1994.

13. National Economic and Social Council, *Ireland in the European Community: performance, prospects and strategy*, Dublin: NESC, 1989.

14. The majority of functions of the Department of Industry and Commerce have subsequently been subsumed by the Department of Enterprise and Employment.

15. *Employment through enterprise*, The response of the Government to the Moriarty Task Force on the implementation of the Culliton Report, Dublin: Stationery Office, 1993.

16. OECD, *Review of national policies for education: Ireland*, Paris: OECD, 1991.

17. See *Education for a changing world*, Green Paper on Education, Dublin: Stationery Office, 1992; National Education Convention Secretariat, *Report on the national education convention*, Dublin: Stationery Office, 1994; *Charting our education future*, op. cit.

18. Evelyn Blennerhassett, Seamus Clince, Niamh Campbell, *Achieving the benefits of information technology in the Irish civil service*, Dublin: Institute of Public Administration, 1992.

19. For a detailed description and review of administrative budgets, see Richard Boyle, *Administrative budgets in the Irish civil service*, Dublin: Institute of Public Administration, 1993.

20. Under the new three-year agreements operating from 1994, it is possible for departments to avoid cuts in their administrative expenditure over the period of the agreement in return for agreement that the department absorb any additional demands made upon it from within its allocation.

21. P.J. Moore, 'Administrative budgets - a new era for civil service managers', *Seirbhís Phoiblí*, Vol. 12, No. 1, 1991, pp. 24-8.

22. *Audits by the Comptroller and Auditor General under section 9 of the Comptroller and Auditor General (Amendment) Act 1993*, note issued by the Comptroller and Auditor General to government departments and offices, 1994.

23. Peter Carvill, 'Things old and new - the Comptroller and Auditor General (Amendment) Act 1993', *Seirbhís Phoiblí*, Vol. 14, No. 2, pp. 38-43.

24. *Audits by the Comptroller and Auditor General under section 9 of the Comptroller and Auditor General (Amendment) Act 1993,* op.cit.

25. Department of Finance, *Framework for the development of a strategic management process in the civil service*, note issued to government departments and offices, 1994.

26. The MSc (Strategic Management - public sector) class of 1993/94, *Strategic management in the Irish civil service: a review drawing on experience in New Zealand and Australia*, University of Dublin, Trinity College, 1994.

27. John Stewart, 'Considerations on strategic management in local government', *Local Government Policy Making*, Vol 17, No. 4, 1991, pp. 62-64.

28. Edward McCumiskey, 'Quality in the civil service', paper presented at Irish Quality Association/Institute of Public Administration conference on public service quality, 9 April 1992.

29. Kevin Murphy, 'Managing the Irish public service in the 1990s', *Seirbhís Phoiblí*, Vol. 14, No. 2, 1993, pp. 7-26.

30. John Mayne, 'Accountability for program performance: a key to effective performance monitoring and reporting', draft paper presented at IIAS Working group on policy and program evaluation, Lyon, May, 1994.

31. Private communication with the Civil Service Commission.

32. The findings in this chapter draw heavily on the interviews conducted with senior civil servants as a part of this study.

33. Henry Mintzberg, 'Rethinking strategic planning part 1: pitfalls and fallacies', *Long Range Planning*, Vol 27, June, 1994, pp. 12 - 21.

34. The MSc. (strategic management - public sector) class of 1993/94, op.cit.

35. For a good discussion on the role of innovation in public service practice, see Peter Sutherland, 'Progress to European union: a challenge for the public service', *Administration*, Vol. 41, No. 2, 1993, pp. 105-119.

36. For a more detailed exploration of this trend, see Boyle, 1995, op.cit.

37. For a general overview of this debate, see Colin Talbot, 'Developing public managers in the UK', *International Journal of Public Sector Management*, Vol. 6, No. 6, 1993, pp. 3-19.

38. For a more detailed discussion on distinctions between private and public sector management, see Boyle, 1995, op.cit.

39. J.M. Kouzes and P.R. Mico, 'Domain theory, an introduction to organisational behaviour in human service organisations', *Journal of Applied Behavioural Science*, Vol.15, No. 4, 1979, pp. 449-69. For a discussion on the use of domain theory in public service analysis in the UK, see Leslie Willcocks and Jenny Harrow (eds), *Rediscovering public services management*, London: McGraw-Hill, 1992.

40. Talbot, op.cit.

41. Taken from D. Ulrick and D. Lake, *Organisational capability*, New York: John Wiley and Sons, 1990.

42. Jerry Carroll, 'Performance appraisal: the civil service experience', *Seirbhís Phoiblí*, Vol. 14, No. 4, 1994, pp. 48 - 58.

43. They are being addressed in the context of the strategic management initiative and the policy direction set in *A government of renewal*, op. cit.

44. See, for example, Bob Garratt, *The learning organisation*, Aldershot: Gower Publishing Co. Ltd. 1982.

45. David A. Garvin, 'Building a learning organisation', *Harvard Business Review*, July-August, 1992, pp. 78-91.

46. Mike Pedler, Tom Boydell and John Burgoyne, 'Towards the learning company', *Management Education and Development*, Vol. 20, No. 1, pp. 1-8.

47. For a discussion on the characteristics of learning organisations, see: Pedler et.al., ibid; and Garvin, op. cit.

48. R. Bruce Dodge, 'Towards a new vision of learning in the public service', *International Journal of Public Sector Management*, Vol. 4, No. 2, 1991, pp. 14-22.

49. Ibid.

BIBLIOGRAPHY

A government of renewal, a policy agreement between Fine Gael, the Labour Party and Democratic Left, Dublin: Stationery Office, 1994

Blennerhassett, E., S. Clince and N. Campbell, *Achieving the benefits of information technology in the Irish civil service*, Dublin: Institute of Public Administration, 1992

Boyle R., *Administrative budgets in the Irish civil service*, Dublin: Institute of Public Administration, 1993

Boyle R., *Towards a new public service*, Dublin: Institute of Public Administration, 1995

Carrol, J., 'Performance appraisal: the civil service experience', *Seirbhís Phoiblí*, Vol. 14, No. 4, 1994, pp. 48-58

Carvill, P., 'Things old and new - the Comptroller and Auditor General (Amendment) Act 1993, *Seirbhís Phoiblí*, Vol. 14, No. 2, 1993, pp. 38-43

Department of Health, *Shaping a healthier future: a strategy for effective healthcare in the 1990s*, Dublin: Stationery Office, 1994

Dodge, R.B., 'Towards a new vision of learning in the public service', *International Journal of Public Sector Management*, Vol. 4, No. 2, 1991, pp. 14-22

Education for a changing world, Green Paper on Education, Dublin: Stationery Office, 1992

Employment through enterprise, The response of the Government to the Moriarity Task Force on the implementation of the Culliton Report, Dublin: Stationery Office, 1993

Garratt, B., *The learning organisation*, Aldershot: Gower Publishing Company Ltd., 1987

Gavin, D.A., 'Building a learning organisation', *Harvard Business Review*, July-August, 1993, pp. 78-91

Gunn, L., 'Public management: a third approach', *Public Money and Management*, Spring/Summer, 1988, pp. 21-25

Hood, C., 'A public management for all seasons?', *Public Administration*, Vol. 69, Spring, 1991, pp. 3-19

Industrial Policy Review Group, *A time for change: industrial policy for the 1990s*, Dublin: Stationery Office, 1992

Kelly, D.J., 'Public administration in a mature democracy', *Administration*, Vol. 41, No. 1, 1993, pp. 72-79

Kouzes, J.M. and P.R. Nico, 'Domain theory, an introduction to organisational behaviour in human service organisations', *Journal of Applied Behavioural Science*, Vol. 15, No. 4, 1979, pp. 449-69

Mintzberg, H., 'Rethinking strategic planning part 1: pitfalls and fallacies', *Long Range Planning*, Vol. 27, June, 1994, pp. 12-21

Moore, P.J., 'Administrative budgets - a new era for civil service managers', *Seirbhís Phoiblí*, Vol. 12, No. 1, 1991, pp. 24-28

National Economic and Social Council, *Ireland in the European Community: performance, prospects and strategy*, Report No. 88, Dublin: NESC, 1989

National Economic and Social Council, *A strategy for the nineties: economic stability and structural change*, Report No. 89, Dublin: NESC, 1993

National Economic and Social Council, *A strategy for competitiveness, growth and employment*, Report No. 96, Dublin: NESC, 1993

OECD, *Review of national policies of education: Ireland*, Paris: OECD, 1991

OECD, *Performance management in government*, Public management occasional paper No. 3, OECD: Paris, 1994

Pedler, M., T. Boydell and J. Burgoyne, 'Towards the learning company', *Management Education and Development*, Vol. 20, No. 1, pp. 1-8

Stewart, J., 'Considerations on strategic management in local government', *Local Government Policy Making*, Vol. 17, No. 4, 1991, pp. 62-64

Sutherland, P., 'Progress to European union: a challenge for the public service', *Administration*, Vol. 41, No. 2, 1993, pp. 105-19

Talbot, C., 'Developing public managers in the UK', *International Journal of Public Sector Management*, Vol. 6, No. 6, 1993, pp. 3-19

Ulrich, D. and D. Lake, *Organisational capability*, New York: John Wiley and Sons, 1990

Willcocks, L. and J. Harrow (eds.), *Rediscovering public services management*, London: McGraw-Hill, 1992